SCOTT BANKSTON

Super Simple Strategy

A simple guide to the stock market to help beginners determine when to buy, sell, or hold a stock for profits

First edition

This book was professionally typeset on Reedsy.
Find out more at reedsy.com

Contents

1

Introduction

Welcome to Super Simple Strategy. My name is Scott Bankston, I am so excited to show you a stock market strategy that is so simple you will wonder why you have not used this strategy before. You probably have never heard of the strategy since there are hundreds of strategies that are used in the stock market. But first, let me tell you a little about myself and why I think I have the experience to write a stock market book. First, let me say the stock market fascinates me. I first became interested in the stock market in 2000. I started out buying stocks and collecting dividends. I couldn't believe I was getting paid for simply owning the stock! Then in 2008 I began to trade options and got more involved in the market. If the year 2008 sounds familiar to you, it's the year of the Housing Crisis where the stock market dropped and the economic forecasts were very bad. At the time, I didn't know a whole lot about the stock market, and I got into the market anyway and lost a lot of money. I wish I hadn't gotten into the market at this time. As a result of losing big money, I was forced to educate myself so this wouldn't happen again. So what

I'm going to teach you are a couple of indicators that will help you make an informed decision about when to buy and sell any stocks you may have. I promise I won't get too involved with this. The stock market can be as complicated as you want it to be but I like to keep this as simple as possible. There are hundreds of books on the stock market but I want this book to be simple! I will show you examples of two indicators in action. Next, I will show you the super simple strategy. Then I will show you the correct stocks to buy for this strategy. I will teach you how to manage your position by teaching you how to calculate the cost basis of the stock and how to add to your position. Does this sound good? If so, stay tuned this is going to be fun!.

2

The Two Behaviors

B efore we get into the book let me explain what the stock market
is and how it works. First stocks are nothing more than a
small piece of the company. Yes, if you buy stocks you own
a small piece of the company. The traders trading the small pieces of
the company are nothing more than human beings buying and selling
stocks and human behavior that never changes. Human behavior will
be the same today as it was 100 years ago and human behavior will be
the same 100 years from now. Stay tuned if you want to find out about
the two human behaviors that drive the stock market

The two behaviors that drive the stock market are *fear* and *greed*. I will
explain these two behaviors and give you a real-life example of these
two behaviors in action.

FEAR

Most people think fear is "Oh no my stock is going down I have to sell my stock." Well, that is some form of fear but there is another form of fear that most people have never heard of but is real and everybody has this form of fear.. It is called the Fear Of Missing Out (FOMO).

Here is how FOMO works in the stock market:

Your friend buys a stock and tells you he bought a stock and it went up $20. You just have to go buy the same stock because you don't want to miss the opportunity. You have the *Fear Of Missing Out*. You have not done one bit of research on the stock but you know you have to have the stock because you do not want to miss the opportunity. Usually, when your FOMO kicks in, like in this example, bad things happen.

Here is how FOMO works in real life example:

I wanted to buy some tickets for a football game. The team was not doing great at the beginning of the season so I hesitated to buy at the price they had listed. Guess what, the next three weeks the team won so I checked the price. OH NO! The price was much higher and the seats were selling fast. I had to get the tickets that day! It was a frantic situation! My FOMO had kicked in big time! Believe me, FOMO is real!

GREED

Every human being has this emotion because everybody wants to make more money. So far, I have never come across anyone that wants to make less money. When one of my stocks goes up to where I can make a nice profit, I always wonder if I could have squeezed out a little more money. Don't think about this! Sell the stock so you can make a nice profit, just be happy with what you got and don't look at it anymore. I will certainly take my own advice.

3

The Overall Market

Here is something most investors do not know. The overall market moves in cycles. The market will move up a while then it will move down. The reasons for these cycles are good and bad economic conditions. Most of the time, it moves up for a long time then a crash comes and moves the market down very quickly. Remember this saying: the market takes the stairs up and the elevator down.

Here is something else about the market you may not know:

When the market moves up or down it takes 75% of the stocks with it. So if the market goes up, 75% of the stocks are going up. If the market moves down 75% of the stocks are going down.

Since you have always heard buy low and sell high, I want to ask you this question. If 75% of the stocks move up with the market, wouldn't you think this would be the best time to make money in the stock market?YES– Buy stocks when the market is moving up! And wouldn't the best time to sell is when the market starts to move down? YES to this question as well.

Let me explain why you don't buy growth stocks when the market is moving down. A lot of growth stocks are not high-quality stocks meaning the company hasn't been around that long and the company does not pay a dividend. So if you buy a stock on the way down, you simply do not know how low the stock will go and an investor can get heart very badly buying when the market is going down. I know this because I bought crappy stocks during the 2008 Housing Crisis. I don't want this pain that I suffered to happen to you.

Keep on reading if you want me to show you a very easy way to tell when the market is going up or down so you will know when to buy or sell your stock.

4

What is an indicator?

The purpose of an indicator is something to help you determine when to buy or sell stock. There are hundreds! I just want to give you a feel for how many indicators there are. The list goes RSI indicator this indicator measures overbought and oversold. Stochastics indicator and MACD indicator. Here are a few more Bollinger bands, ichimoku cloud, keltner channel, and Fibonacci Retracements. My goodness there are so many and I only listed a few. Thank goodness for this strategy. For long-term buying and holding, you only need two indicators and they are simple!

First Indicator:

200-day simple moving average

The 200-day simple moving average (SMA) is a long-term moving average and simply uses the closing price of the stock or index. A line is drawn from one day's closing price to the next day's closing price. So as the 201st day closes, the day that was way back to the first day drops off. When the 202nd day closes, the second day way back will drop off and this will continue. The 200-day SMA is a very slow indicator. It takes 200 days to get data from this indicator.

Second Indicator:

The second indicator is a 50-day simple moving average (SMA). This indicator is a shorter-term indicator and uses the closing price of a stock or index. And just like the 200-day indicator, the 50-day SMA is a line drawn from one day's closing price to the next day's closing price. So you probably can guess what happens with this Indicator. When the 51st day closes, the first day drops off. When the 52nd day, closes the 2nd day drops off. Only these two indicators will be used to show you this strategy. The 50-day SMA is a much faster indicator than the 200-day SMA. It takes 50 days to get data from this indicator.

In the next chapter, I will show you how to use the two indicators as a buy and sell signal.

5

Buy Signal

The Golden Cross:

When using these two indicators the 200-day SMA indicator is a longer-term moving average and the 50-day SMA is the shorter-term moving average. The 50-day SMA will cross above the 200-day SMA forming what is called a *Golden Cross*. I have seen two strong Golden Crosses formed within the last few years. I will show you examples of both.

BUY SIGNAL

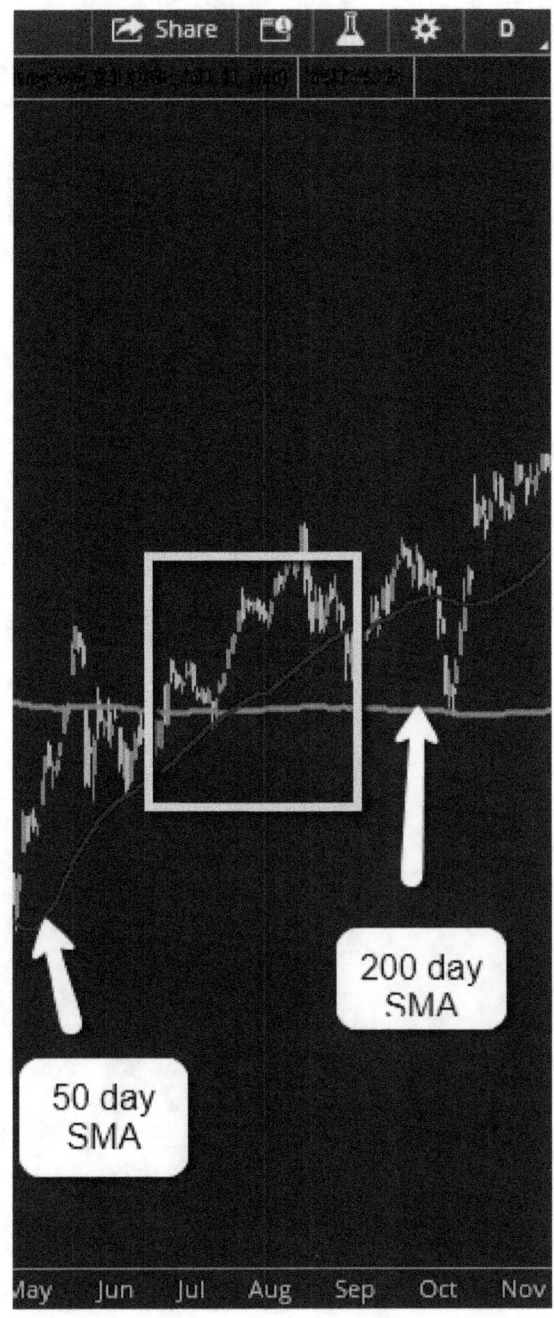

This Golden Cross was formed in 2009 right after the housing crisis was coming to an end.

The screenshot to the left is from the Housing Crash of 2008. After the market quit coming down, it formed a Golden Cross that is inside the box. Notice how the 50-day SMA crosses above the red 200-day SMA. Look at what happens to the stock or index. It moves up!

Now let's look at a more recent example. This is from the Covid Crash of 2020.

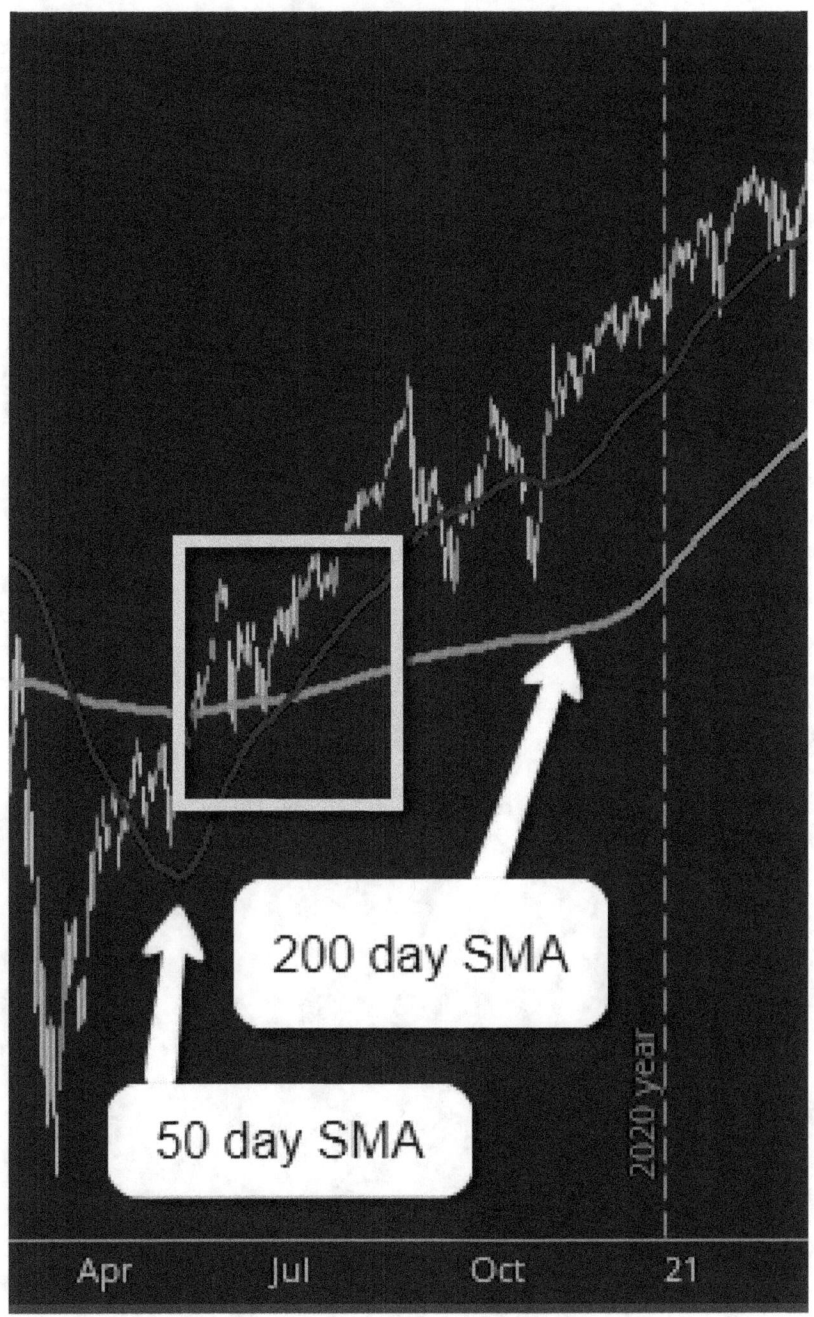

Again notice the Golden Cross formed inside the box. See how the 50-day SMA crosses above the red 200-day SMA. The stock or index moves up once the Golden Cross is formed. That's why it's called a Golden Cross.

If you see a Golden Cross form, it is time to buy stock!

6

Sell Signal

The Death Cross:

Death Cross occurs when the 50-day SMA crosses below the 200-day SMA. Here I will use examples from the same two events the Housing Crash of 2008 and the Covid Crash of 2020 respectively.

The Death cross occurs when the 50-day SMA crosses below the 200-day SMA. This is highlighted in the box. Look at what happens to the stock or index, it moves down. If you remember the rule from Chapter 2, *75% of all stocks will follow the direction of the market.*

This will drag down 75% of all the stocks. Yuck!

I am going to show two examples of the Death Cross then show you in Chapter 7 that sometimes the Death Cross is not such a bad thing if you buy high-quality stocks that pay dividends. But first our next example.

Here is what the Death Cross of the Housing Crash looked like way back in 2007. It didn't look like much at first but this innocent little death cross went on to become the 2008 housing crisis, and it got nasty! OUCH!

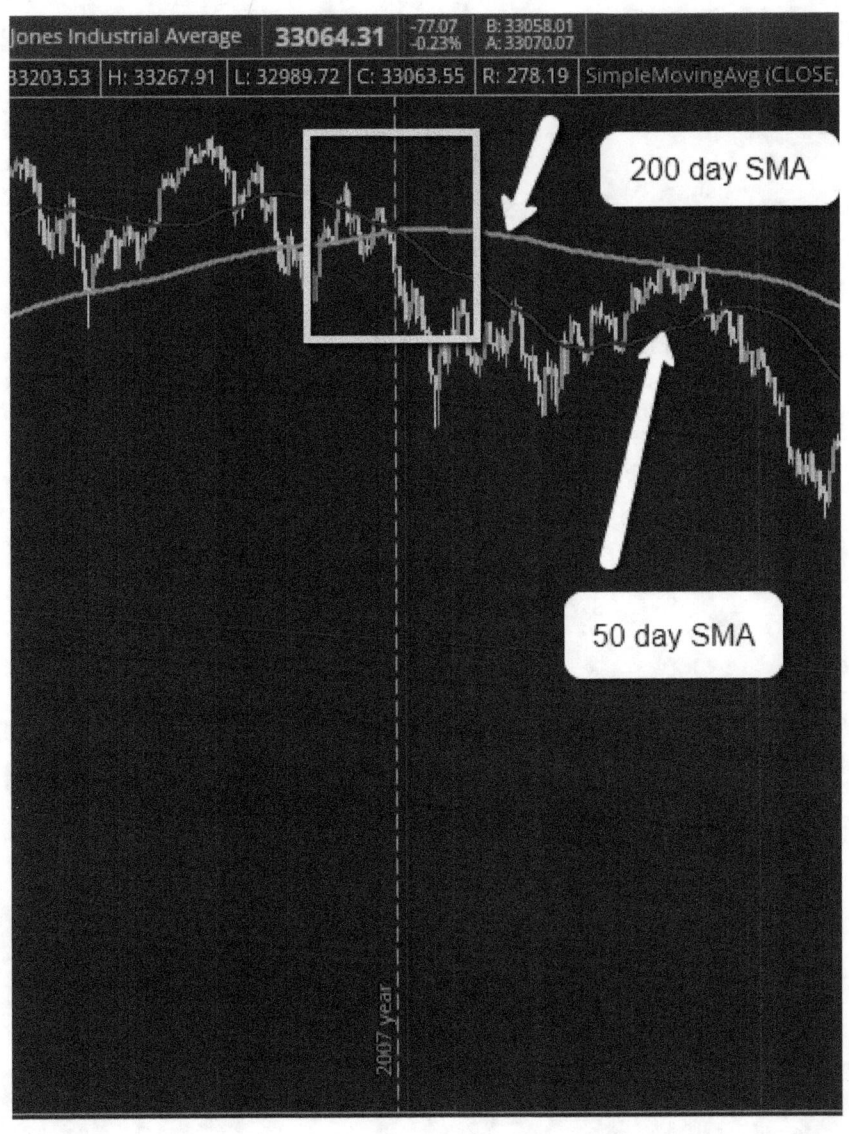

Notice how the 50-day SMA crosses below the 200-day SMA and the Death Cross was formed. And again, look at what happens to the stock or index. It drops and that is how the term Death Cross came about.

Now I want to show you an example of a severe Death Cross. This Death Cross is from the 2020 Covid Crash. Wow, look how fast this stock went down. Most buy-and-hold investors would have needed more time to get their stock out before the market pushed the stock down. If you were an investor who could not get your stock out, don't worry I'm going to show you how to manage these stocks. Stay tuned!

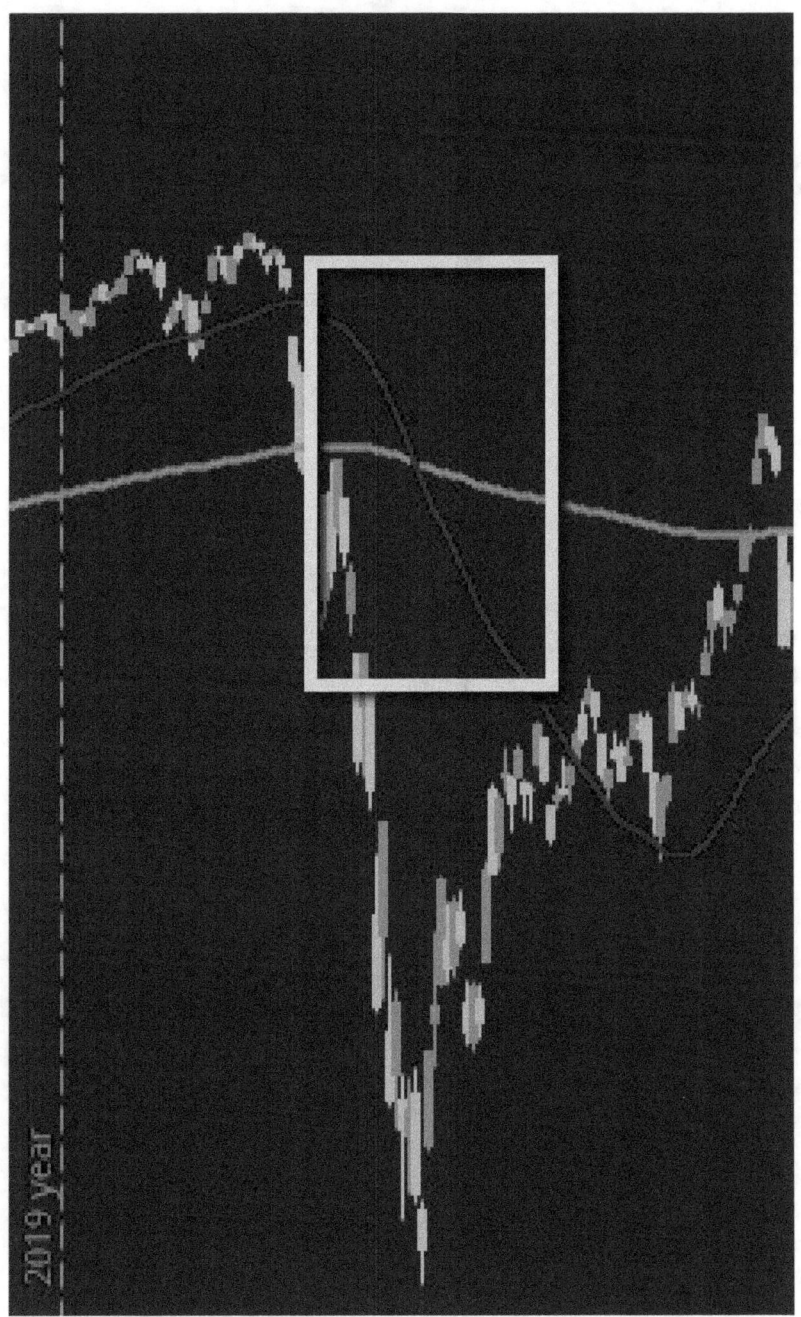

2019 year

7

The Bigger Picture

I have used screenshots from the Dow Jones Industrial Index. I have used close-up screenshots of the different crosses of the 2008 Housing Crash and the 2020 Covid Crash but I have not shown you the entire overall picture of how the Golden Cross and the Death Cross can help you buy and sell stock.

First here is the big picture of the 2008 Housing Crash.

The first observation and the biggest is when a Death Cross forms a Golden Cross will form as well. In this example, it took over a year for the Golden Cross to form but It did form. And why do you think a Golden Cross always forms? Remember the stock market is made up of human beings and human thought never changes. The stock has simply been pushed down to a price where investors want to buy the stock. Yeah, it's kind of like the black Friday sale at Walmart!

The second thing we notice is if you had stocks in this market between the Death Cross and the Golden Cross they would have been pushed down hard! I remember this, there were a lot of people that lost a lot of money during this time because they were buy-and-holders and had to sell the stock for retirement. Some people might say don't worry the stock market will recover. Maybe it will but some people did not have the time for the market to recover. And some stocks did recover but some stocks certainly did not. And know this, stocks are nothing more than a small piece of the company. If the economy were so bad during the crisis, maybe the company wouldn't survive. You must buy stock in a good strong company that can survive a terrible crisis like the Housing Crisis of 2008. The people who lost money simply did not know when to sell their stock especially if they were getting close to retirement. After reading this and understanding Death Crosses and Golden Crosses, you will now have a better understanding of when to buy stocks when a Golden Cross is formed and sell stocks when a Death Cross is formed.

Next, we are going to look at the 2020 Covid Crisis. You will notice this crash is a bit different.

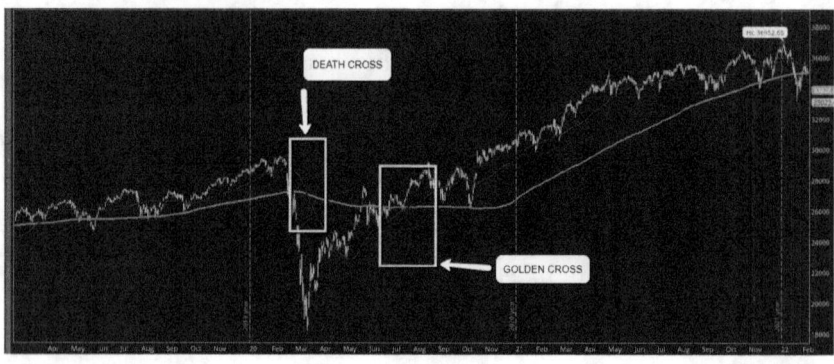

The first thing we can conclude from this big picture of the 2020 Covid Crash is wow the Death Cross formed very quickly and it went down fast. It was a hard quick crash and here's why. Most long-term investors don't have a clue when or if they want to sell the stock. So their fear takes over and they rush to sell the stock. This rush is what causes the stock to drop so fast. I'm willing to bet most long-term investors could not even get to a broker fast enough to sell their stocks.

The second thing we can observe is…wow the Golden Cross was formed very quickly it sure went up fast. However, unless you had a crystal ball you wouldn't have known where the eventual bottom was going to be. The stock's drop could have been much more severe but at the time nobody knew where the stock was going to stop dropping. Hindsight is crystal clear and the quick recovery is easy to see now. Since the Death Cross and the Golden Crosses were formed so quickly, it would be very hard for the average long-term investor to get their stocks sold so they probably would have just left the stock in the market. As previously discussed, we didn't know at the time how much the market was going to push the stock down. So that brings me to another way to manage the stock if another crash comes. And it most certainly will! In the next chapter, I will discuss how to manage the stock that gets crushed by the market.

8

The Strategy

The first thing I want to discuss is the types of stocks I want you to buy. You want to buy stocks of strong companies that pay a dividend. In long-term investing, dividends are the name of the game.

Let me explain what a dividend is and why they are so important. Dividends are monies paid to the stockholder every three months just for owning the stock. The more stocks you own the more dividends, money you get. So as a long-term investor, you are trying to accumulate more and more stocks. Sometimes dividends are paid monthly and sometimes every six months. It really depends on the company. I can't tell you which stocks to buy because I want you to do the work to research this out. There are many books to help you with picking high-quality stocks. But know this, don't become dividend blind. Dividend blind is when a dividend is so huge you can't believe how much the company is paying out. If you come across this, do some more research on the company. I do know that distressed companies will try to make things look great just to get you to buy the stock. Then after you purchase the stock you find out the company is close to going bankrupt. You don't want this!

Now I want to show you how to manage a stock during a Death Cross situation to show you how to get more stock. As previously discussed, 75% of stocks go with the overall market. A Death Cross pushes the market down. This is an excellent time to "go shopping" for some high-quality nice dividend-paying stocks.

We are going to have to do some mathematical calculations for this. I am going to show you how to determine the cost basis of your stock. The cost basis is the average price you paid for the stock. Finding the cost basis is helpful if you made several buys of the stock at different prices. Here is how it works:

Say you bought 25 shares of Apple (AAPL) at $150 per share. This would cost you $3750. And remember AAPL does pay a dividend. A Death Cross comes and pushes the stock down. AAPL is now $100 a share and you decide to spend another $3750. You have now bought 37.50 shares of AAPL and your cost basis has just dropped from $150 a share to $120 a share. The Death Cross is still pushing down on AAPL and you decide to buy another $3750 but AAPL is pushed down to $75 a share so now you can buy 50 shares. The new cost basis is $100 per share. AAPL is still going down and you were able to invest another $3750 and make a purchase at $50 a share. You now have purchased 75 shares. Which brings the cost basis of your share to $80 per share.

Here is what the buys of AAPL look like in mathematical form:

$150 * 25 = $3750
$100 * 37.50 = $3750
$75 * 50 = $3750
$50 * 75 = $3750

187.5 $15000

# of total
shares
purchased

Total
amount
used to
purchase
stock

So the way you find the cost basis in a stock is to take the total amount of the money invested and divide by the number of shares. In this example $15000 / 187.8 = $80. So you have lowered your cost by $70 from your initial buy.

Do you understand how a down market can help you buy more shares? And more shares equal more dividends.

You can do this with any stock. Also, a term you might have heard is buy the dip. This term means when the stock goes down, buy some more stock. It is okay to buy the dip if you have a strong stock that pays a good dividend. This is a great way to accumulate more shares. And again more shares equals more dividends and more dividends equals more money. And while you are accumulating more and more stocks, There is another way you can use these dividends to accumulate even more stocks, It's called the *dividend reinvestment program* (DRIP). How the dividend reinvestment program works is instead of getting the cash for the dividends you can get the dividends reinvested to purchase more stocks. It might be fractions of a share but it will begin to accumulate very quickly. As long as you are still working, the dividend reinvestment program can be an excellent way to grow your wealth. Yes, a long-term dividend strategy is a fantastic way to accumulate wealth.

I personally did this with a company called Philip Morris. Back in 2002, the company owned the cigarette part and they also owned Kraft. So I began to watch this stock and every time they had a court decision where the company had to pay out millions, I noticed the stock would drop. So I began to make my purchases every time the stock dropped and I had my dividends reinvested to purchase more stocks.. I started to accumulate more stock and every time I noticed the cost basis would go down. I had a good bit accumulated and sold it during the 2008 Housing Crash. As I look back I wish I hadn't sold. I let my fear take over! I didn't know about fear and greed back in 2008. I didn't know about Death Crosses and Golden Crosses but I wish I did. I sure didn't understand how to figure out the cost basis of a stock and lost a lot of money as a result of not knowing this basic information. So I hope you can use this information in this book to go out and hopefully help you make better decisions in the stock market.

Here is a story about my mother who taught me about the stock market. My mother, as a young woman, would make small buys here and there of AT&T stock. Then it would split for more shares (sorry I didn't explain a split in this book). She would buy some more shares then it would split again. She would get the dividends reinvested. She ended up with 3896 shares! After she retired, she would get the dividends paid to her every three months. My goodness, how fantastic it was to get an extra $1200 just for owning a stock. And she had other stocks too! My point with this story about my mother is to let you know anybody can do this dividend strategy. I hope a young person finds this book and begins to invest. And eventually ends up through the years getting paid huge dividends. I think up in heaven my mother would have a smile on her face.

9

Conclusion

Y ou now know a very simple buy-and-hold strategy and two basic indicators. As I said before, I didn't want to get too technical or involved with this because I didn't want you to become overwhelmed with all this stock market stuff. I want you to use the indicators to help you make better decisions. Remember, buy high-quality stocks that pay nice dividends. Have the dividends reinvested through the years and when you retire you can use the dividends for extra income. That pretty much sums up the strategy. Thank you for purchasing this book. Please leave me an honest review, I sure would appreciate it.

About the Author

Scott Bankston has been investing in the market since 2000. He started with buy-and-hold strategies and moved to more advanced ones involving calls and puts. Scott always has the novice investor in mind and tries to explain the strategies in the simplest form.